Slippers
Knitting and Felting

Learn to Make Cute and Cozy Footwear for All Ages

Sabine Abel • Annette Diepolder • Karoline Hoffmeister

Landauer Publishing

Contents

The Perfect Slippers   3

Techniques   **4**
Knit Felting How-To   5

Projects   **13**
Spotty Slipper   16
Inspired by Asia   20
Softly Striped   24
Stylish Understatement   26
Autumn Leaves   30
Cheeky, Cheerful, Colorful   34
Buttoned Up   38
Warm, Warmer, Warmest   42
A Star is Born   44
Tone on Tone   50
Triple Mélange   54
Sophisticated Checks   58

Blue and Purple with Polka Dots   62
Father's Day   64
Pastel Magic   68
Mary Janes   74
Ballerinas   76
Checks in Blue   80
Sweet Kitten   84
Little Bear   86
Happy Bunny   88
Puppy Slippers   90
Love Bug   92
Index   95

Abbreviations

ch	chain stitch(es)
dc	double crochet
sc	single crochet
sl st	slip stitch(es)

The Perfect Slippers

These knitted felt slippers always keep our feet toasty and warm.

Even better—these slippers are easy to make because they are knitted in a similar way to socks. The basic shape is simple, just an oversized sock. Using thick needles and knit and purl stitches, knitting is quick and easy. Irregularities in the stitch pattern are completely irrelevant, as they are no longer visible after felting. Once the slippers have been knitted, the washing machine does the rest of the work, matting and shrinking the project to the right size.

Whether made in stripes, stars, or polka dot patterns, or decorated with pom-poms or ruffles, these individual slippers are popular with the whole family and are always a welcome gift.

TECHNIQUES

Knit Felting How-To

The Yarn

Chunky 100% wool yarn is quick to knit and felts easily in the washing machine.

The Knitting Needle

The wool yarn is knitted with circular knitting needles and double-pointed needles, each with a needle size of US 10.5–11 (7–8mm).

Gauge

To ensure that the slippers correspond to the desired size after felting, it is advisable to first make and felt a gauge for each project. After all, different types of washing machines and settings can result in different degrees of shrinkage.

The dimensions of the gauge before and after felting are given for each project.

1. Cast on at least 1.5x as many stitches as specified for the 4" (10.2cm) width **before washing**, and also knit around 1.5x as many rows as specified.

2. Place the measuring tape or a stitch counter under the stitches **before washing**, and count the stitches to a length of 4" (10.2cm). Place it next to the stitches and count the rows to 4" (10.2cm). Do not to place the tape measure on the edge but in the middle of the knitted fabric; the edge stitches will distort the result.

3. It is no longer possible to count stitches after felting. Instead, measure the length and width of the outer edges of the knitted fabric and make note of both the measurements and the total number of stitches and rows.

4. **After felting,** pull the test piece into shape and measure the length and width. Calculate the number of stitches per 4" (10.2cm): divide the total number of (knitted) stitches by the width of the piece. For example, you have knitted 37 stitches, and the piece is felted 8 ½" wide: 37:8.5 = 4.352, i.e. about 4.4 stitches per inch = 18 stitches per 4" in width. Calculate the height in the same way. For example, you noted 46 rows, and the piece is 8" high: 46:8 = 5.8 rows per inch = 23 rows per 4" in height. For the metric conversion of these examples, see page 7.

5. If the gauge is smaller than specified **after felting**, it has been worked too tightly, and it is advisable to use a slightly thicker needle. If it turns out larger than stated, the knitting was looser, and a slightly thinner needle could be used.

Don't be confused by the fact that your slippers seem to look way too big when knitting—when washed, i.e. matted, they shrink a lot (around a third). The result is a piece of knitting in which the individual stitches are almost indistinguishable.

Felting in the Washing Machine

Wash the knitted projects in the washing machine on the warm setting, usually around 104°F (40°C). Make sure to note the information on the yarn band, and repeat the washing process if necessary. When washed, the wool becomes denser and firmer.

Any detergent is suitable for felting, but liquid detergent is best as it leaves no residue in the form of small granules. Always wash the knitted items together with some towels or something similar. The friction with the other pieces increases the felting process. Rubber washing balls that agitate the clothes for cleaning also support the felting process by rolling the laundry. The washing machine should be no more than two-thirds full.

While the slippers are still damp, shape them, stuff them with newspaper, and let them dry.

TIP

Use the felted stitch samples as coasters or sew them together to make a patchwork pillow. You can also make small, decorative gift tags from them.

Note

If the slippers are still too big after felting, simply wash them again at 104°F or 140°F (40°C or 60°C), depending on how much the item needs to shrink. If the slippers turn out too small after felting, they can be pulled into shape or stretched while they are still wet.

Useful Tips!

Liquid Latex

Liquid latex can be applied to the soles of your slippers to make them nonslip.

Needle Felting

Details can also be worked into the slippers for decoration, using the needle-felting technique. The fibers of needle-felting wool (such as fairy tale wool) or fibers of wool yarn can be pulled apart and felted with a needle. Felting needles are made of steel and have fine barbs at the tip.

The needle penetrates far through the wool with each stitch. For safety reasons, a piece of foam should always be used as a base. The base should be at least 2" (5.1cm) thick; a household sponge is sufficient for smaller sections, but a block of foam is ideal for larger parts. The wool is shaped into the desired shape. Then prick it with the needle as often as necessary until the wool has compacted to the desired firmness.

Keep Separated

Place small knitted or crocheted pieces, such as pom-poms and flowers, in a mesh laundry bag for felting; or put them in a nylon stocking and tie it. Each small item should be placed in an individual laundry bag or nylon stocking. Alternatively, put them together in a nylon stocking, but then tie a knot in the stocking between the individual parts; otherwise, the pieces will become matted together.

Slippers with Heel Seam

Tools & Materials:
- Yarn for felting, super bulky weight: for amount, see table or instructions
- Circular knitting needle, US 10.5–11 (7–8mm)
- Double-pointed needles, US 10.5–11 (7–8mm)
- Tapestry needle

Stockinette stitch: Knit stitches on the right side and purl stitches on the wrong side.

Stockinette stitch in rounds: Knit all stitches.

Knit 2 stitches out of 1 stitch: Purl 1 stitch, do not let the stitch slip off the left needle yet, but place the working yarn to the back, insert the stitch again from the back (right side interlaced), pick up the yarn, and now let the stitch slip off the needle.

Gauge:
Stockinette stitch with 10.5–11 (7–8mm): 12 stitches and 16 rows = 4" x 4" (10.2 x 10.2cm) before felting; 3" x 3" (7.6 x 7.6cm) after felting.

Instructions

The slippers are started at the heel and knitted in stockinette stitch according to the table on page 9.

Cast on the desired number of stitches with the circular knitting needle, see row (**A**). Knit the number of rows given in the table in stockinette stitch, see row (**B**). On the last row from the back, double the first and last stitches on the row and knit 2 stitches out of 1 stitch.

Continue working the foot in rounds: Distribute the stitches evenly over the four needles of the double-pointed needles, form a round, and knit in the round the number of stitches given in the table, see row (**C**).

After the specified number of rounds, see row (**D**), knit the first 2 stitches of each needle together for the tip in each round until there are only 8 or 10 stitches left.

Cut the working thread and pull it through the remaining stitches with the wool needle. Pull it together tightly and sew the thread. Close the heel seam: double the cast-on edge and sew the edges together. Make sure that the seam is flat and that the thread is not pulled too tight; otherwise, the seam will shrink too much during felting.

Felt the slippers with a few towels and some detergent in the washing machine on the warm or hot setting, depending on the yarn (follow the yarn label and in the project instructions). After washing, pull the slipper into shape and push out the heel. Stuff with paper to dry.

> **TIP**
>
> The slippers can also be customized. For example, if you want them to be longer than stated in the table, simply knit 3 additional rows for ½" (1.3cm) extra length. Simply knit 3 rows less for shorter shoes.

Slippers with Heel Seam (100% virgin wool, 55 yds [50ml]/1.75oz [50g])

Gauge: stockinette stitch with 10.5–11 (7–8mm): 12 sts and 16 rows = 4" x 4" (10.2 x 10.2cm) before felting

	US Size (UK Size)	Kids 9/10.5 (8/9)	Kids 11.5/12.5 (10/11)	Kids 13/1 (11.5/12.5)	Kids 1.5/2 (13/13.5)	Kids 3/3.5 (2/2.5)	Women 5/6 (3/4)	Women 7/8 (5/6)	Women 9/10 (7/8)	Men 8/9 (7/8)	Men 10/11 (9/10)	Men 12/13 (11/12)
A	Number of cast-on stitches	24	26	26	28	30	30	32	34	36	38	40
B	Number of rows	22	23	24	25	28	31	33	35	37	39	41
	Stitch increase in the last back row					2 stitches = increase 1 stitch on each side						
C	Number of stitches in rounds	26	28	28	30	32	32	34	36	38	40	42
D	Rounds to beginning of tip	20	21	22	23	24	25	27	29	31	32	34
	Total foot length after felting	7" (17.8cm)	7½" (19.1cm)	7⅞"–8¼" (20–21cm)	8⅔" (22cm)	8⅔"–9" (22–22.9cm)	9½"–9⅞" (24.1–25.1cm)	10¼"–10⅔" (26–27.1cm)	11"–11½" (27.9–29.2cm)	11½"–11⅞" (29.2–30.2cm)	11⅞"–12¼" (30.2–31.1cm)	12¼"–12⅔" (31.1–32.2cm)
	Yarn needed per pair			3.5oz (100g)				5.3oz (150g)			7.1oz (200g)	

Slippers with Cap Heel

Tools & Materials:
- Yarn for felting, super bulky weight: for amount, see table or instructions
- Circular knitting needle, US 10.5–11 (7–8mm)
- Double-pointed needles, US 10.5–11 (7–8mm)
- Tapestry needle

Stockinette stitch: Knit stitches on the right side and purl stitches on the wrong side.

Stockinette stitch in rounds: Knit all stitches.

Gauge:
Stockinette stitch with 10.5–11 (7–8mm): 12 stitches and 16 rows = 4" x 4" (10.2 x 10.2cm) before felting; 3" x 3" (7.6 x 7.6cm) after felting.

Instructions
The slippers are knitted in stockinette stitch according to the chart on page 11. To do this, cast on the number of stitches corresponding to the desired size, see row **(AA)**. Knit the indicated number of rows for the heel wall height in stockinette stitch, see row **(BB)**. Divide the stitches for the heel cap into three parts, see row **(CC)**.

Knit the stockinette stitch only over the stitches in the middle third, while also knitting the outer stitches of the side parts as follows: On the right side, knit the last stitch of the middle third twisted together with the following stitch of the side section. Turn and purl the first stitch. On the wrong side, purl the last stitch of the middle third together with the following stitch of the side part. Turn work and slip the first stitch knitwise.

Continue like this until only the middle third stitches remain.

Continue knitting in rounds for the foot from the sides of the heel wall in the first round, see row **(DD)**, by casting on the required number of stitches for the upper foot, see row **(EE)**. Knit stitches from the second side of the heel wall again, see row **(DD)**. Cast the stitches evenly on four double-pointed needles and knit the specified number of rounds over all stitches to the beginning of the tip, see row **(GG)**.

Then work the tip: Knit the first 2 stitches on each needle together on each round. If there is 1 stitch more on two needles than on the other two, to equalize the number of stitches, work the first round of decreases only on these two needles, see row **(HH)**, then knit the indicated rounds of decrease according to the table, see row **(II)**. Cut the working thread and pull it through the remaining stitches with the wool needle. Pull tightly together and sew the thread.

Felt the slippers with a few towels and some detergent in the washing machine on the warm or hot setting, depending on the yarn (follow the yarn label and in the project instructions). After washing, pull it into shape and push out the heel. Stuff with paper to dry.

Slippers with Cap Heel (100% virgin wool, 55 yds [50m]/1.75oz [50g])

Gauge: stockinette stitch with 10.5–11 (7–8mm): 12 sts and 16 rows = 4" x 4" (10.2 x 10.2cm) before felting

	US Size (UK Size)	Kids 9/10.5 (8/9)	Kids 11.5/12.5 (10/11)	Kids 13/1 (11.5/12.5)	Kids 1.5/2 (13/13.5)	Kids 3/3.5 (2/2.5)	Women 5/6 (3/4)	Women 7/8 (5/6)	Women 9/10 (7/8)	Men 8/9 (7/8)	Men 10/11 (9/10)	Men 12/13 (11/12)
AA	Cast-on stitches	26	26	28	30	30	32	32	34	36	38	38
BB	Heel wall height rows	13	13	14	15	15	16	17	17	18	18	20
CC	Heel cap stitches	10/6/10	10/6/10	11/6/11	12/6/12	12/6/12	12/8/12	12/8/12	13/8/13	13/10/13	14/10/14	14/10/14
DD	Continue from this stitch	9	9	10	11	11	11	11	12	12	13	13
EE	Upper foot cast-on stitches	4	4	4	4	4	4	4	4	4	4	4
FF	Total stitches	28	28	30	32	32	34	34	36	38	40	40
GG	Rounds to beginning of tip	18	19	19	23	24	26	27	29	30	32	34
HH	Equalize stitch count (1st round of decreases)	0	0	0	0	0	2	2	0	2	0	0
II	Decrease rounds	5	5	6	6	6	6	6	7	7	8	8
	Total foot length after felting	7" (17.8cm)	7½" (19.1cm)	7⅞"–8¼" (20–21cm)	8⅔" (22cm)	8⅔"–9" (22–22.9cm)	9½"–9⅞" (24.1–25.1cm)	10¼"–10⅔" (26–27.1cm)	11"–11½" (27.9–29.2cm)	11½"–11⅞" (29.2–30.2cm)	11⅞"–12¼" (30.2–31.1cm)	12¼"–12⅔" (31.1–32.2cm)
	Yarn needed per pair		3.5oz (100g)				5.3oz (150g)				7.1oz (200g)	

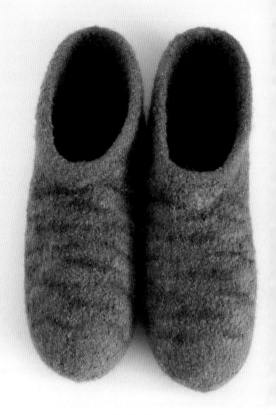

PROJECTS

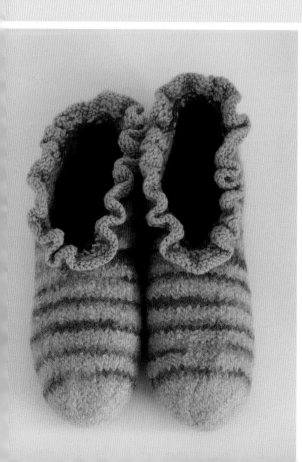

Spotty Slipper

Size: Women 7–10 (UK 5–8) and Men 8–10 (UK 7–9)

Tools & Materials:

- Yarn for felting, super bulky weight
  Shown here: Lana Grossa Feltro (100% virgin
  wool; 55 yds [50m]/1.75oz [50g]): 7.1oz (200g)
  in dark gray mottled (color 04), and 3.5oz
  (100g) in Bordeaux (color 15) or pink (color
  38)
- Knitting needles, US 10.5 (7mm) and US 13
  (9mm)
- Espadrilles soles
- Textile glue, super glue, or hot glue
- Tapestry needle
- Twine or thick thread

Gauge:

Stockinette stitch with 13 (9mm): 9.5 stitches and
13.5 rows = 4" x 4" (10.2 x 10.2cm) before felting.
Sole material: 18" x 19 ¾" (45.7 x 50.2cm), before
felting; 12 ½" x 12 ½" (31.8 x 31.8cm), after felting.

Stockinette stitch: Knit all stitches on the right side
and purl all stitches on the wrong side.

Moss stitch: Knit 1 stitch and purl 1 stitch
alternately, staggering the pattern by 1 stitch on
each row.

Edge stitch: Slip the first stitch of each row, knit the
last stitch of each row.

Polka dot pattern: Work according to the counting
pattern. Both right side and wrong side rows are
shown. Knit 1 x 30 stitches in width and 1 x 36 rows
in height. Cross the threads at all color transitions.

Instructions

For the **soles** (the felt fabric will be cut later), with US
13 (9mm) needles, cast on a total of 44 stitches in
dark gray mottled, and knit 19 ¾" (50cm) in
stockinette stitch. Then cast off the stitches.

For the **slipper top** (work twice), with US 10.5
(7mm) needles, cast on 30 stitches in Bordeaux or
pink, and knit 3 rows in the moss stitch. Then work
the 36 rows of the polka dot pattern according to
the chart, knitting in the dots in dark gray mottled
and using a separate small ball for each dot. Then
cast off all stitches.

Finishing Off

Felt all parts in the washing machine on the warm setting, according to the instructions (page 6). After washing, pull it into shape and let it dry flat. Cut the outline of the **soles** from the dark gray mottled felt material. Coat the espadrille soles with glue, and place the fabric on them to fit exactly. Press firmly and weigh down with books.

Cut the **tops** of the shoes from the two dotted, felted rectangles. To do this, use the template included with the soles. Choose the right shoe size. The edge facing the foot is the edge with a moss stitch and forms the finish. Add about ½" (1.3cm) for the seam on the curve and cut the top. Sew to the sole of the espadrilles using twine or another thick thread.

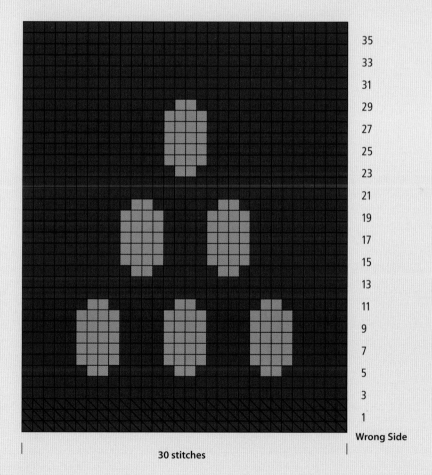

35
33
31
29
27
25
23
21
19
17
15
13
11
9
7
5
3
1

Wrong Side

30 stitches

▨ = 1 moss stitch in Bordeaux or pink
▦ = 1 stockinette stitch in Bordeaux or pink
▢ = 1 stockinette stitch in dark gray mottled

Inspired by Asia

Size: Women 8 (UK 6)

Tools & Materials:

- Yarn for felting, super bulky weight
  Shown here: Lana Grossa Feltro (100% virgin wool; 55 yds [50m]/1.75oz [50g]): 3.5oz (100g) in salmon (color 83) and 1.75oz (50g) in beige (color 24)
- Knitting needles, US 10.5–11 (7–8mm)
- Crochet hook, US J-10 (6mm)
- Espadrilles soles
- Tapestry needle
- 2 tassel caps
- Twine or thick thread
- Textile glue, super glue, or hot glue

Gauge:
Stockinette stitch with 10.5–11 (7–8mm): 12 stitches and 16 rows = 4" x 4" (10.2 x 10.2cm), before felting; 3" x 3" (7.6 x 7.6cm), after felting.

Stockinette stitch: Knit all stitches on the right side and purl all stitches on the wrong side.

Embroidery motif: Work according to the counting pattern. Both right side and wrong side rows are shown. Embroider the motif before felting as described in the instructions.

1 slip-knit-pass: Slip 1 stitch knitwise, knit 1 stitch, then pass the slip stitch over.

1 double slip-knit-pass: Slip 1 stitch knitwise, knit 2 stitches together, then pass the slip stitch over.

Edge stitch: Knit the first and last stitch of each row.

Instructions

For the **top**, with US 10.5–11 (7–8mm) needles, start at the curved toe and work to the toe of the shoe: cast on 3 stitches in salmon and work 1 row of purl stitches (wrong side). Knit in stockinette stitch without edge stitches, on both sides, in every other stitch. Increase row 3 x 1 stitch and 1 x 2 stitches, then cast on 1 x 7 stitches on each side = 27 stitches.

Now work edge stitches on both sides. In the Row 26, decrease 1 stitch on both sides as follows: edge stitch, knit 2 stitches together, knit 21 stitches, 1 slip-knit-pass, edge stitch. Work these decreases 4 more times in every other row, then decrease 1 more time in every other row as follows: edge stitch, knit 3 stitches together, knit 9 stitches, 1 double slip-knit-pass, edge stitch. Repeat the decrease 1 more time in the following row. Cast off the remaining 9 stitches. Work the **second top** in the same way.

Finishing Off

With a US 10 (6mm) crochet hook, crochet the tip and cast-on edge (= 27 sts in total) in beige with 1 row of sc and 1 row of reverse stockinette stitches (= sc from left to right). Then embroider the motif according to the chart with beige yarn in the middle of the stitch on both sides.

Felt both tops in the washing machine on the warm setting, according to the instructions (page 6). After washing, pull it into form and shape the crocheted edge, especially shaping the 3 stitches at

the cast on to a point. Using the twine and tapestry needle, sew the tops to the soles of the espadrilles.

To make the **tassel**, wrap the salmon yarn several times around your left index and middle fingers, spreading them slightly. Tie off the threads on one side and cut the threads on the other side. On the tied side, glue the threads into the tassel cap with glue, and work the second tassel in the same way. After the drying time, cut the threads evenly back to around 1" (2.5cm). Sew one tassel to the top center of each slipper.

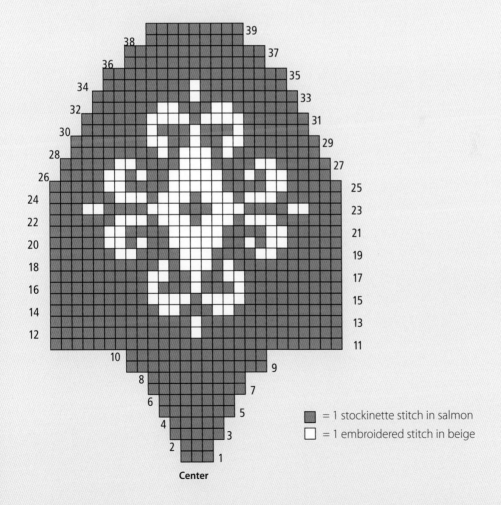

■ = 1 stockinette stitch in salmon
□ = 1 embroidered stitch in beige

Center

Softly Striped

Size: Women 5–6 (UK 3–4)

Using the Heel Seam table (page 9), the slippers can also be made in other sizes. The yarn consumption would change accordingly.

Tools & Materials:
- Yarn for felting, bulky weight
  Shown here: buttinette Woll Butt Felting Wool (100% virgin wool, 55 yds [50m]/1.75oz [50g]): 3.5oz (100g) each in off-white (color 99.219.26) and mauve (color 99.129.64)
- Circular knitting needles, US 10.5–11 (7–8mm)
- Double-pointed knitting needles, US 10.5–11 (7–8mm)
- Tapestry needle
- Crochet hook, US L-11 (8mm)

Stockinette stitch: Knit stitches on the right side and purl stitches on the wrong side.

Stockinette stitch in rounds: Knit all stitches.

Stripe sequence: *2 rounds of off-white, 1 round of mauve, repeat from * onward.

Gauge:
Stockinette stitch with 10.5–11 (7–8mm): 12 stitches and 16 rows = 4" x 4" (10.2 x 10.2cm), before felting; 3" x 3" (7.6 x 7.6cm), after felting.

   Note: Work according to Slippers with Heel Seam (page 8). However, fewer stitches are initially cast on, then the number of stitches is increased as described until the required number of stitches is reached.

Instructions

Using the circular knitting needle, cast on 18 stitches in mauve and knit 16 rows in stockinette stitch. Then knit another 12 rows in stockinette stitch, increasing 1 stitch in every 2 rows, until there are 30 stitches on the needles in Row 28 **(A)**. Knit another 2 rows in stockinette stitch over these 30 stitches, doubling the first and last stitches on the last row from the back = 32 stitches **(C)**. Distribute the stitches evenly over four needles on the double-pointed needles (= 8 stitches per needle), close the work in the round, change to off-white, and knit 25 rounds in stockinette stitch **(D)**.

Work the **tip** in stockinette stitch in off-white according to the basic instructions: On each round, knit the first 2 stitches on each needle together until only 8 stitches remain. Note: Depending on the size, there can also be 10 stitches at this point. Cut the working thread, pull it through the remaining stitches, pull it together tightly, and sew it off. Close the heel seam as described.

Crochet 1 round of sc in off-white along the top edge of the slipper. For the edge of the tip in the next round, work 3 ch and 3 dc in 1 stitch, *pass over 2 stitches, 1 sc in the 3rd stitch, 3 chain sts, and 3 dc. Repeat from * until the edge has been crocheted around once. Work the **second slipper** in the same way.

Finishing Off

Felt the slippers in the washing machine on the hot setting, according to the instructions (page 6). Pull into shape after washing. Stuff with paper to dry.

Stylish Understatement

Size: Women 9–10 (UK 7–8)

Using the Cap Heel table (page 11), the slippers can also be made in other sizes. The yarn consumption would change accordingly.

Tools & Materials:

- Yarn for felting, bulky weight
  Shown here: buttinette Woll Butt Felting Wool (100% virgin wool, 55 yds [50m]/1.75oz [50g]): 3.5oz (100g) each in off-white (color 99.219.26) and anthracite (color 99.219.36)
- Circular knitting needles, US 10.5–11 (7–8mm)
- Double-pointed knitting needles, US 10.5–11 (7–8mm)
- Tapestry needle

Stockinette stitch: Knit stitches on the right side and purl stitches on the wrong side.

Stockinette stitch in rounds: Knit all stitches.

Garter stitch: Knit all stitches on the right and wrong sides.

Gauge:

Stockinette stitch with 10.5–11 (7–8mm): 12 stitches and 16 rows = 4" x 4" (10.2 x 10.2cm), before felting; 3" x 3" (7.6 x 7.6cm), after felting.

Note: Work according to Slippers with Cap Heel (page 10).

Instructions

With the circular knitting needle, cast on 34 stitches in off-white **(AA)** and knit 17 rows in stockinette stitch for the heel wall **(BB)**. Then work the heel cap in anthracite according to the basic instructions **(CC)**. Now work in the round, picking up 12 stitches on each side of the heel wall **(DD)** and casting on 4 new stitches over the foot **(EE)**. Then for the foot, knit the 36 stitches **(FF)** in stockinette stitch in anthracite in rounds. After 25 rounds, switch to off-white and knit 4 more rounds in off-white = 29 rounds **(GG)**.

Work the **tip** in off-white according to the basic instructions: On each round, knit the first 2 stitches on each needle together until only 8 stitches remain, **(HH)** and **(II)**. Cut the working thread, pull it through the remaining stitches with the wool needle, and sew it off.

Pick up 36 stitches from the upper edge of the slipper in anthracite with the circular knitting needle and knit a total of 4 zigzags over 9 stitches in garter stitch as follows: knit the first and last 2 stitches of each zigzag together 3 times in every 2 rows (Row 6 = 3 stitches). With the remaining 3 stitches, work a double slip-knit-pass (= slip 1 stitch, knit 2 stitches together, and pass the slipped stitch over). Work the **second slipper** in the same way.

Finishing Off

Sew the threads and felt the slippers in the washing machine on the hot setting, according to the instructions (page 6). Pull into shape after washing. Stuff with paper to dry.

TIP

This project can be reworked in all sizes. Please note that an odd number of stitches must be used for the points on the edge of the shoe. The zigzags can then be knitted using fewer stitches using the same principle, which can also result in five or six points.

Autumn Leaves

Size: Women 7–8 (UK 5–6)

Using the Heel Seam table (page 9), the slippers can also be made in other sizes. The yarn consumption would change accordingly.

Tools & Materials:

- Yarn for felting, bulky weight
  Shown here: buttinette Woll Butt Felting Wool (100% virgin wool, 55 yds [50m]/1.75oz [50g]): 3.5oz (100g) each in beige (color 99.115.53) and autumn (color 99.219.40)
- Yarn, super fine weight
  Shown here: buttinette Woll Butt Socke Sock Yarn, 6-ply (75% virgin wool/25% polyamide, 142 yds [130m]/1.75oz [50g]): 1.75oz (50g) in tangerine (color 99.271.49)
- Circular knitting needles, US 10.5–11 (7–8mm), 24" (61cm) long
- Double-pointed knitting needles, US 6 (4mm) and US 10.5–11 (7–8mm)
- Crochet hook, US G-6 (4mm)

Stockinette stitch: Knit stitches on the right side and purl stitches on the wrong side.

Stockinette stitch in rounds: Knit all stitches.

Garter stitch: Knit all stitches on the right and wrong sides.

Garter stitch in rounds: Work 1 round of knit stitches and 1 round of purl stitches alternately.

Gauge:
Stockinette stitch with 10.5–11 (7–8mm): 12 stitches and 16 rows = 4" x 4" (10.2 x 10.2cm), before felting; 3" x 3" (7.6 x 7.6cm), after felting.

Note: Work according to Slippers with Heel Seam (page 8).

Instructions

With the US 10.5–11 (7–8mm) circular knitting needle, cast on 32 stitches in autumn (A). Knit in stockinette stitch as follows: 3 rows in autumn, *2 rows in beige, 4 rows in autumn. Repeat from * until 33 rows are reached (B), double the first and last stitches when working the last row on the wrong side = 34 stitches (C). Distribute the stitches on four needles (8-9-8-9 sts), close the piece in the round, and work in stockinette stitch as follows: *4 rounds of beige, 2 rounds of autumn, and repeat from * onward.

After 27 rounds (D), work the **tip** in stockinette stitch according to the basic instructions: On each round, knit the first 2 stitches on each needle together until only 10 stitches remain. **Note:** Depending on the size, there can only be 8 stitches at this point. Cut the working thread, pull it through the remaining stitches, and close the heel seam as described.

Crochet the top edge with sc in tangerine (approx. 36 stitches). Close to the round, finish the work and cut the thread. Using the double-pointed needles, pick up new stitches ⅛" (3.2mm) from the top edge in tangerine and knit 1 stitch out of the front and back loops of each stitch = 18 stitches per needle or 72 stitches in total. In the following round, double each stitch (= knit each stitch once from the front and once from

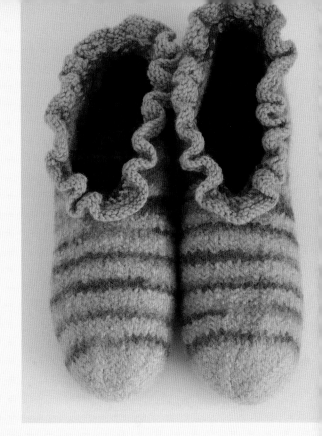

the back on the right, then lift it off the left needle). Now knit 4 rounds in garter stitch, then loosely cast off all stitches. Close the heel seam as described. Work the **second slipper** in the same way.

Finishing Off

Sew the threads and felt the slippers in the washing machine on the hot setting, according to the instructions (page 6); the super fine yarn does not become felted. Pull into shape after washing. Stuff with paper to dry.

Cheeky, Cheerful, Colorful

Size: Women 7–8 (UK 5–6)

Using the Heel Seam table (page 9), the slippers can also be made in other sizes. The yarn consumption would change accordingly.

Tools & Materials:

- Yarn for felting, bulky weight
  Shown here: buttinette Wool Butt Felting Wool (100% virgin wool, 55 yds [50m]/1.75oz [50g]): 7.1oz (200g) in mixed (color 99.115.51) and 1.75oz (50g) in light green (color 99.228.16)
- Circular knitting needles, US 10.5–11 (7–8mm)
- Double-pointed knitting needles, US 10.5–11 (7–8mm)
- Crochet hook, US L-11 (8mm)
- Pom-pom maker
- Tapestry needle

Stockinette stitch: Knit stitches on the right side and purl stitches on the wrong side.

Stockinette stitch in rounds: Knit all stitches.

Gauge:

Stockinette stitch with 10.5–11 (7–8mm): 12 stitches and 16 rows = 4" x 4" (10.2 x 10.2cm), before felting; 3" x 3" (7.6 x 7.6cm), after felting.

   Note: Work according to Slippers with Heel Seam (page 8).

Instructions

With the US 10.5–11 (7–8mm) circular knitting needle, cast on 32 stitches in mixed **(A)** and knit 33 rows in stockinette stitch **(B)**, doubling the first and last stitches in the last back row = 34 stitches **(C)**. Distribute the stitches on four needles (8-9-8-9 sts), join the work in the round, and knit 27 rounds in stockinette stitch **(D)**.

Work the **tip** in light green according to the basic instructions: On each round, knit the first 2 stitches on each needle together until only 10 stitches remain. Note: Depending on the sizes, there can only be 8 stitches at this point. Cut the working thread, pull it through the remaining 10 stitches, and close the heel seam as described.

Crochet the top edge of the slipper with 2 rounds of sc in light green. Work 3 sc in each corner. Work the **second slipper** in the same way.

Finishing Off

Sew the threads and felt the slippers in the washing machine on the hot setting, according to the instructions (page 6). Pull into shape after washing. Stuff with paper to dry. Wrap 2 pom-poms with a diameter of 2" (5.1cm) in light green and sew 1 pom-pom in the middle of each slipper.

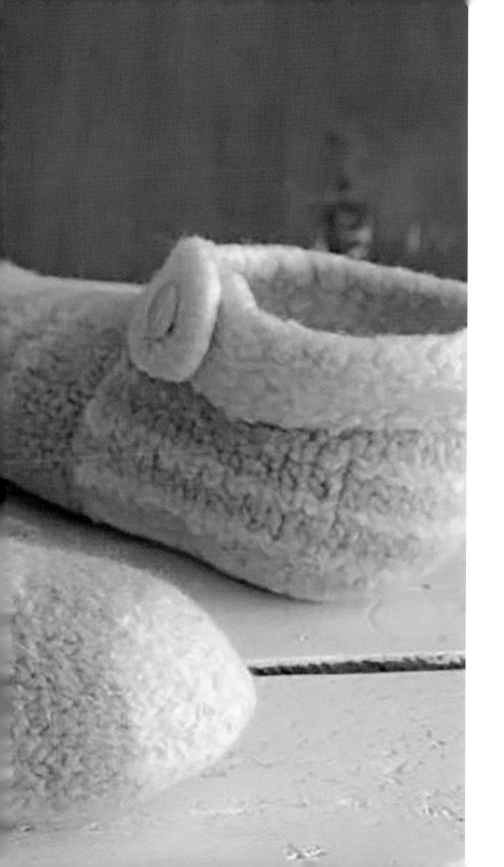

Buttoned Up

Size: Women 7–8 (UK 5–6)

Using the Cap Heel table (page 11), the slippers can also be made in other sizes. The yarn consumption would change accordingly.

Tools & Materials:

- Yarn for felting, super bulky weight
  Shown here: Wolle Rödel Strick & Filzwolle (100% virgin wool, 55 yds [50m]/1.75oz [50g]): 3.5oz (100g) each in off-white and mint
- Circular knitting needles, US 10.5–11 (7–8mm)
- Double-pointed knitting needles, US 10.5–11 (7–8mm)
- Tapestry needle
- 2 buttons

Stockinette stitch: Knit stitches on the right side and purl stitches on the wrong side.

Stockinette stitch in rounds: Knit all stitches.

Stripe sequence heel wall: *2 rows of mint, 2 rows of off-white, and work from * 4 times, ending with 1 row of off-white (= 17 rows).

Stripe sequence foot: 6 rounds of mint, *2 rounds of off-white, 2 rounds of mint, work from * 3 times, 2 rounds of off-white, and 6 rounds of mint (= 26 rounds).

Small moss stitch: Knit 1 stitch, purl 1 stitch alternately. Stagger the pattern by 1 stitch on each row.

Gauge:

Stockinette stitch with 10.5–11 (7–8mm): 12 stitches and 16 rows = 4" x 4" (10.2 x 10.2cm), before felting; 3" x 3" (7.6 x 7.6cm), after felting.

Note: Work according to Slippers with Cap Heel (page 10).

Instructions

With the circular knitting needle, cast on 32 stitches in mint (AA) and knit 17 rows in stockinette stitch in the stripe sequence for the heel wall (BB). Then work the heel cap in off-white according to the basic instructions (CC). Work in the round, picking up 11 stitches on each side of the heel wall (DD) and casting on 4 new stitches over the foot (EE).

For the foot, knit the 34 stitches (FF) in stockinette stitch in rounds, continuing the stripe sequence. After 27 rounds in the stripe sequence (GG), continue working the stitches on the double-pointed needles (8-9-8-9 sts), and work the tip according to the basic instructions in off-white: In each round, knit the first 2 stitches of each needle together until there are only 8 stitches left, (HH) and (II). Cut the working thread, pull it through the remaining stitches with the wool needle, and sew it off.

Cast on 38 stitches from the upper edge of the slipper in wool white, and cast on 9 more stitches for the strap at the end. Note: For other sizes, adjust this number of stitches individually. Knit 5 rows in moss stitch over these stitches, working the buttonhole on Row 5 on the strap (= knit 3 stitches, cast off 3 stitches, knit the remaining stitches on the row. In the following row, cast on the slipped stitches again). After a total of 8 rows, cast off all stitches.

Work the second slipper in the same way, only work the strap in the opposite direction. To do this, first cast on 9 stitches and then pick up 38 stitches from the edge of the shoe.

Finishing Off

Sew the threads and felt the slippers in the washing machine on the hot setting, according to the instructions (page 6). Pull into shape after washing. Stuff with paper to dry. After drying, sew the buttons onto the strap to match the buttonhole.

Warm, Warmer, Warmest

Size: all sizes, see Heel Seam table (page 9)

Tools & Materials:
- Yarn for felting, super bulky weight
  Shown here: Lana Grossa Feltro (100% virgin wool; 55 yds [50m]/1.75oz [50g]): olive (color 21) or heather (color 69)
- Yarn, super bulky weight
  Shown here: Lana Grossa Mille II (50% virgin merino wool/50% polyacrylic, 60 yds [55m]/1.75oz [50g]): 1.75oz (50g) each in raw white (color 17), and anthracite (color 68) or smoke blue (color 123)
- Knitting needles, US 8 (5mm) and US 10.5–11 (7–8mm)

Stockinette stitch: Knit stitches on the right side and purl stitches on the wrong side.

Stockinette stitch in rounds: Knit all stitches.

Ribbed pattern in rounds: Knit 2 stitch, purl 2 stitch alternately.

Stripe sequence for version 1: *5 rounds of off-white, 5 rounds of anthracite, and work from * 4 times = 40 rounds.

Stripe sequence for version 2: *8 rounds in smoke blue, 8 rounds in off-white, work from * 2 times, and finish the cuff with 8 rounds in smoke blue = 40 rounds.

Gauge:
Stockinette stitch with 10.5–11 (7–8mm): 12 stitches and 16 rows = 4" x 4" (10.2 x 10.2cm), before felting; 3" x 3" (7.6 x 7.6cm), after felting.

Note: Work according to Slippers with Heel Seam (page 8).

Instructions

Work a pair of slippers with a heel seam in the desired size according to the basic instructions; knit in olive for version 1 and in heather for version 2. Close the back seam with a stitch, but do not felt the shoes yet.

For the cuff, knit 24 stitches (up to Kids size 3.5 [UK 2.5]) or 28 stitches (for Women sizes 5–10 [UK 3–8]) or 32 stitches (for Men sizes 8–12 [UK 7–11]) evenly distributed from the edge using US 8 (5mm) needles in off-white for version 1, or smoky blue for version 2. Work the waistband in rib pattern in the respective stripe sequence. Then loosely cast off all stitches.

The gaps between the stitches close during subsequent washing, as the shoe shrinks during felting, but the cuff retains its size due to the polyacrylic content of the yarn. Work the second slipper in the same way.

Finishing Off

Weave in the loose ends and felt the slippers in the washing machine on the warm setting, according to the instructions (page 6). Pull into shape after washing. Stuff with paper to dry.

A Star is Born

Size: Women 7–8 (UK 5–6)

Using the Heel Seam table (page 9), the slippers can also be made in other sizes. The yarn consumption would change accordingly.

Tools & Materials:

- Yarn for felting, super bulky weight
  Shown here: Lana Grossa Feltro (100% virgin wool; 55 yds [50m]/1.75oz [50g]): 5.3oz (150g) in heather (color 69) or dark olive (color 86), and 1.75oz (50g) in dark olive (color 86) or lilac (color 99)
- Knitting needles, US 10.5–11 (7–8mm)
- Double-pointed knitting needles, US 10.5–11 (7–8mm)
- Liquid latex (optional)

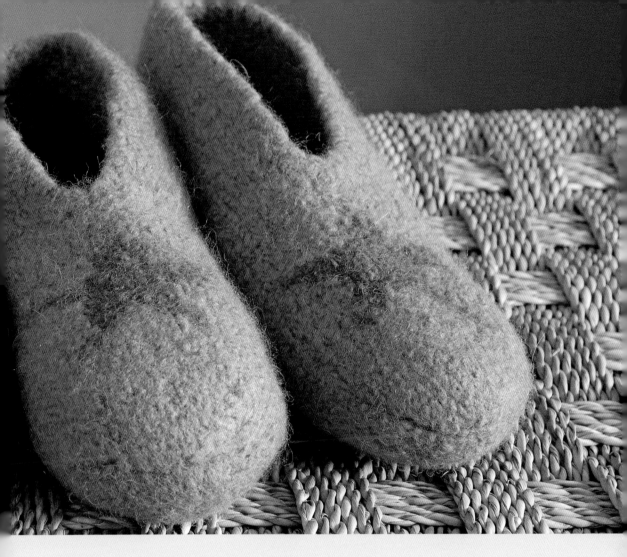

Stockinette stitch: Knit stitches on the right side and purl stitches on the wrong side.

Stockinette stitch in rounds: Knit all stitches.

Edge stitch: Always knit the first and last stitch of each row on the right.

Star motif: Knit stockinette stitch according to the chart: Work the Small Star for sizes Kids 13–2 and Women 5–8 (UK 11.5–6) and the Large Star for sizes Women 9–10 and Men 8–13 (UK 7–12). Knit the motif over 11 [13] stitches and 16 [20] rounds/rows using the intarsia technique in the contrasting color. Use one ball for each colored area. Cross the threads at all color transitions.

Gauge:
Stockinette stitch with 10.5–11 (7–8mm): 12 stitches and 16 rows = 4" x 4" (10.2 x 10.2cm), before felting; 3" x 3" (7.6 x 7.6cm), after felting.

   Note: Work according to Slippers with Heel Seam (page 8).

A Star is Born

Instructions

With the US 10.5–11 (7–8mm) circular knitting needle, cast on 32 stitches in the respective main color **(A)** and work 33 rows in stockinette stitch with edge stitches on both sides **(B)**, doubling the first and last stitches in the last wrong side = 34 stitches **(C)**.

Close the stitches in the round and distribute them on three double-pointed needles: half of the stitches are on needle 1, and one quarter of the stitches are on needles 2 and 3. Mark the round transition between needle 1 and needle 2 for the right shoe and between needle 3 and needle 1 for the left shoe.

Knit 6 rounds, then embroider the star according to the chart. With an even number of stitches on needle 1, there is 1 stitch more behind the star on the right shoe and 1 stitch more in front of the star on the left shoe. Depending on the size, knit the first 3 rounds of the Small Star or the first 4 rounds of the Large Star according to the chart. Continue working the motif on the wrong and right sides so that no long tension threads are created. For the later seam, double the last stitch of needle 3 on the left shoe and the first stitch of needle 2 on the right shoe = 1 increase.

When the motif is finished, close the stitches again to form a round, knit the previously increased stitch together, and knit 5 more rounds in the main color = 27 rounds. Note: For other sizes, work the star in the middle of the number of rounds up to the tip **(D)**, so for smaller sizes, work fewer rounds before and after the knit-in pattern; for larger sizes, work more rounds if necessary.

Distribute the stitches on four needles on the double-pointed needles (= 8-9-8-9 sts), and work the **tip** in stockinette stitch according to the basic instructions in the main color: In each round, knit the first 2 stitches of each needle together until there are only 10 stitches left. Note: Depending on the sizes, there can only be 8 stitches at this point. Cut the working thread, pull it through the remaining stitches, pull it together tightly, and sew it off. Close the heel seam as described. Work the **second slipper** in the same way.

Finishing Off

Weave in the loose ends and felt the slippers in the washing machine on the warm setting, according to the instructions (page 6). Pull into shape after washing. Stuff with paper to dry.

Optional: Coat the soles with liquid latex to achieve an anti-slip effect.

Large Star Chart

Sizes: Women 9–10 and Men 8–13 (UK 7–12)

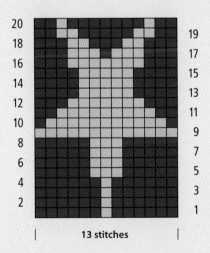

13 stitches

Little Star Chart

Sizes: Kids 13–2 and Women 5–8 (UK 11.5–6)

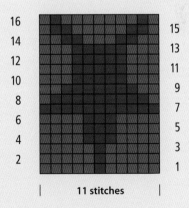

11 stitches

■ = 1 stockinette stitch in dark olive
■ = 1 stockinette stitch in lilac
■ = 1 stockinette stitch in heather

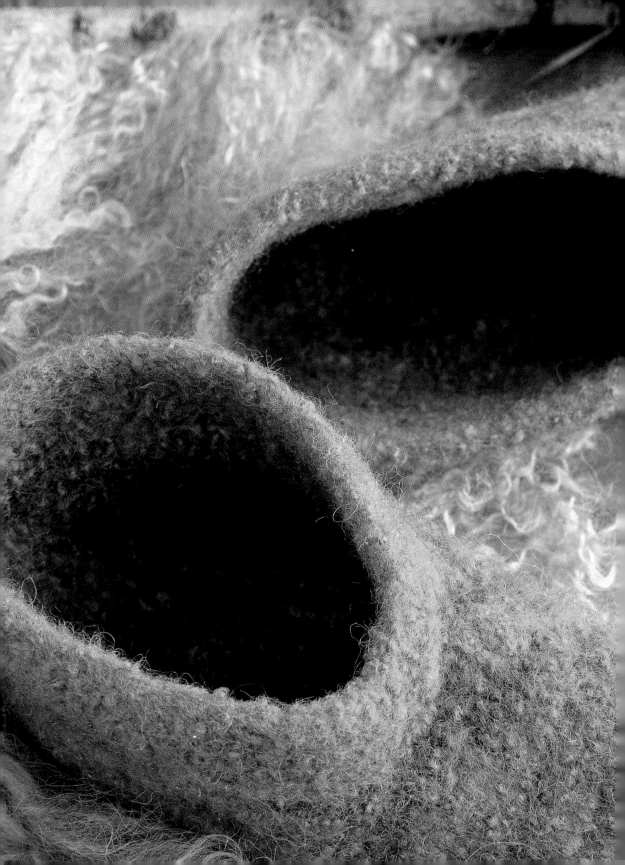

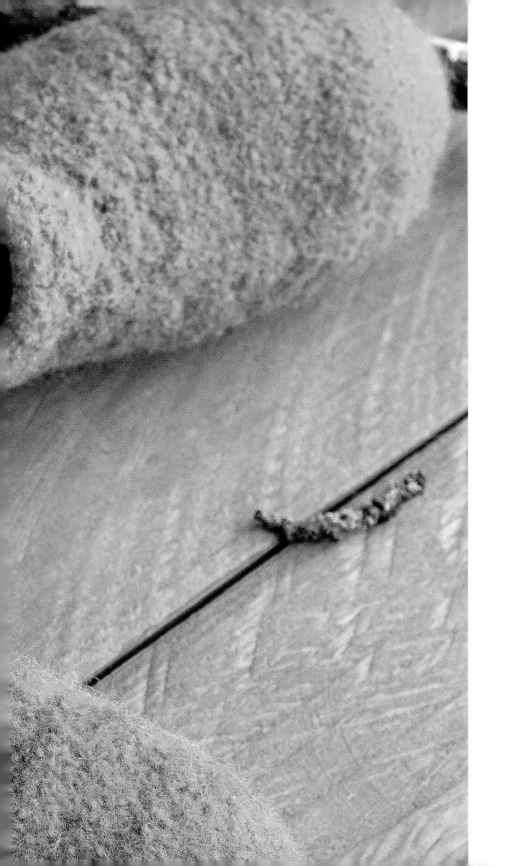

Tone on Tone

Size: Men 12–13 (UK 11–12)

Using the Cap Heel table (page 11), the slippers can also be made in other sizes. The yarn consumption would change accordingly.

Tools & Materials:

- Yarn for felting, bulky weight
  Shown here: buttinette Wool Butt Felting Wool (100% virgin wool, 55 yds [50m]/1.75oz [50g]): 3.5oz (100g) each in petrol (color 99.219.33) and petrol mottled (color 99.233.43)
- Circular knitting needles, US 10.5–11 (7–8mm)
- Double-pointed knitting needles, US 10.5–11 (7–8mm)
- Crochet hook, US L-11 (8mm)
- Tapestry needle

Stockinette stitch: Knit stitches on the right side and purl stitches on the wrong side.

Stockinette stitch in rounds: Knit all stitches.

Stripe sequence: *2 rows/rounds in petrol mottled, 2 rows/rounds in petrol, and repeat from * onward.

Gauge:

Stockinette stitch with 10.5–11 (7–8mm): 12 stitches and 16 rows = 4" x 4" (10.2 x 10.2cm), before felting; 3" x 3" (7.6 x 7.6cm), after felting.

Note: Work according to Slippers with Cap Heel (page 10).

Instructions

With the circular knitting needle, cast on 38 stitches in petrol mottled **(AA)** and knit 20 rows in stockinette stitch for the heel wall in the stripe sequence **(BB)**. Work the heel cap in petrol mottled according to the basic instructions **(CC)**.

Work in rounds, picking up 13 stitches from each side of the heel wall **(DD)** and casting on 4 new stitches over the foot **(EE)**. Distribute the 40 stitches **(FF)** for the foot over four needles of the needle set (= 10 stitches per needle), join in the round and knit 34 rounds in stockinette stitch **(GG)**.

Work the **tip** in petrol, according to the basic instructions: On each round, knit the first 2 stitches on each needle together until only 8 stitches remain, **(HH)** and **(II)**. Cut the working thread, pull it through the remaining stitches with the wool needle, and sew it off. Crochet the top edge of the slipper in petrol with 1 round of sc. Work the **second slipper** in the same way.

Finishing Off

Sew the threads and felt the slippers in the washing machine on the hot setting, according to the instructions (page 6). Pull into shape after washing. Stuff with paper to dry.

Triple Mélange

Size: Women 9–10 (UK 7–8)

Using the Heel Seam table (page 9), the slippers can also be made in other sizes. The yarn consumption would change accordingly.

Tools & Materials:
- Yarn for felting, super bulky weight
  Shown here: Lana Grossa (100% wool; 55 yds [50m]/1.75oz [50g]): 5.3oz (150g) Feltro Chess in natural/light gray/medium gray/gray green/violet blue (color 838), or Feltro Line in white/light gray/medium gray/light blue/cornflower (color 438), or Feltro Print in gray purple/lilac/ nougat/smoke blue (color 395)
- Circular knitting needles, US 10.5–11 (7–8mm)
- Double-pointed knitting needles, US 10.5–11 (7–8mm)
- Liquid latex (optional)

Stockinette stitch: Knit stitches on the right side and purl stitches on the wrong side.

Stockinette stitch in rounds: Knit all stitches.

Gauge:
Stockinette stitch with 10.5–11 (7–8mm): 12 stitches and 16 rows = 4" x 4" (10.2 x 10.2cm), before felting; 3" x 3" (7.6 x 7.6cm), after felting.

  Note: Work according to Slippers with Heel Seam (page 8). Work each version in one color using the specified yarn.

Instructions
With a US 10.5–11 (7–8mm) circular needle, cast on 34 stitches (A) and knit 35 rows stockinette stitch (B), doubling the first and last stitch when working the last row on the wrong side = 36 stitches (C). Distribute the stitches evenly over four needles on the double-pointed needles (9 stitches per needle), close the work in the round, and knit 29 rounds in stockinette stitch (D).

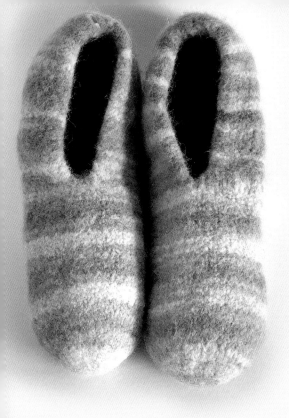

Work the **tip** according to the basic instructions:
On each round, knit the first 2 stitches on each
needle together until only 10 stitches remain.
    Note: Depending on the size, there can also be 8
stitches at this point. Cut the working thread, pull it
through the remaining stitches, and close the heel
seam as described.

Finishing Off

Sew the threads and felt the slippers in the washing
machine on the warm setting, according to the
instructions (page 6). Pull into shape after washing.
Stuff with paper to dry.
    Optional: Coat the soles with liquid latex to
achieve an anti-slip effect.

Sophisticated Checks

Size: Women 9–10 (UK 7–8)

Using the Heel Seam table (page 9), the slippers can also be made in other sizes. The yarn consumption would change accordingly.

Tools & Materials:
- Yarn for felting, super bulky weight
  Shown here: Lana Grossa Feltro Uni (100% wool; 55 yds [50m]/1.75oz [50g]): 3.5oz (100g) each in denim blue (color 101) and light beige (color 102)
- Circular knitting needles, US 10.5–11 (7–8mm)
- Double-pointed knitting needles, US 10.5–11 (7–8mm)
- Liquid latex (optional)

Stockinette stitch: Knit stitches on the right side and purl stitches on the wrong side.

Stockinette stitch in rounds: Knit all stitches.

Slip stitch pattern in rounds: Number of stitches divisible by 4. Work according to the chart. All rounds are noted. Always repeat Rounds 1–4.

Slip stitch pattern in rows: Number of stitches divisible by 4 + 2 stitches. Work according to the chart. All rows are noted. Always repeat Rows 1–4. The first and last stitch of each row are always knitted as edge stitches in the color of the respective row. Depending on the size, if the number of stitches cannot be divided evenly, the excess stitches are knitted in C1 at the beginning of the row after the edge stitch and at the end of the row before the edge stitch. In the round, the stitches are knitted as the first or last stitch of the round in C1.

Color 1 (C1) = denim blue, **Color 2 (C2)** = light beige.

Gauge:
Stockinette stitch with 10.5–11 (7–8mm): 12 stitches and 16 rows = 4" x 4" (10.2 x 10.2cm), before felting; 3" x 3" (7.6 x 7.6cm), after felting.
   Note: Work according to Slippers with Heel Seam (page 8).

Instructions

With the US 10.5–11 (7–8mm) circular knitting needle, cast on 34 stitches in denim blue **(A)** and knit 35 rows as follows **(B)**: Purl 1 row on the wrong side and knit 2 rows on the right side, then work 32 rows in slip stitch pattern according to the knitting chart, doubling the first and last stitch in the last row on the wrong side = 36 stitches **(C)**. Distribute the stitches on four needles (9 stitches per needle), join the work in the round and knit 29 rounds in the slip stitch pattern **(D)**.

Work the **tip** in C1 according to the basic instructions: In each round, knit the first 2 stitches of each needle together until there are only 10 stitches left. Note: Depending on the sizes, there can only be 8 stitches at this point. Cut the working thread, pull it through the remaining stitches, and close the heel seam as described. Work the second slipper in the same way.

Finishing Off

Weave in the loose ends and felt the slippers in the washing machine on the warm setting, according to the instructions (page 6). Pull into shape after washing. Stuff with paper to dry.

Optional: Coat the soles with liquid latex to achieve an anti-slip effect.

Slip Stitch Chart in Rows

Row 4 in C2

Row 3 in C2

Row 2 in C1

Row 1 in C1

| 4 stitches |

Always repeat Rows 1–4.

Slip Stitch Chart in the Round

Round 4 in C2
Round 3 in C2
Round 2 in C1
Round 1 in C1

| 4 stitches |

Always repeat Rounds 1–4.

Color 1 (C1) = denim blue
Color 2 (C2) = light beige

☐ = 1 knit

⊟ = 1 purl

▣ = slip 1 stitch purlwise with the thread behind the work

▣ = slip 1 stitch purlwise with the thread in front of the work

Blue and Purple with Polka Dots

Size: Women 7–8 (UK 5–6)

Using the Cap Heel table (page 11), the slippers can also be made in other sizes. The yarn consumption would change accordingly.

Tools & Materials:

- Yarn for felting, bulky weight
  Shown here: buttinette Wool Butt Felting Wool (100% virgin wool, 55 yds [50m]/1.75oz [50g]): 3.5oz (100g) each in light blue (color 99.129.65) and plum (color 99.102.84)
- Circular knitting needles, US 10.5–11 (7–8mm)
- Double-pointed knitting needles, US 10.5–11 (7–8mm)
- Crochet hook, US L-11 (8mm)
- Tapestry needle
- Blue and purple felting wool
- Felting needle, medium or fine
- Household sponge

Stockinette stitch: Knit stitches on the right side and purl stitches on the wrong side.

Stockinette stitch in rounds: Knit all stitches.

Gauge:
Stockinette stitch with 10.5–11 (7–8mm): 12 stitches and 16 rows = 4" x 4" (10.2 x 10.2cm), before felting; 3" x 3" (7.6 x 7.6cm), after felting.

    Note: Work according to Slippers with Cap Heel (page 10).

Instructions

Using the circular knitting needle, cast on 32 stitches in light blue **(AA)** and knit 17 rows in stockinette stitch for the heel wall **(BB)**. Work the heel cap in light blue according to the basic instructions **(CC)**. Continue knitting in the round on double-pointed needles for the foot, picking up 11 stitches on the sides of the heel wall as described **(DD)** and casting on 4 stitches for the upper foot **(EE)** = 34 stitches **(FF)**. Distribute the stitches on four needles (= 8-9-8-9 sts), changing to plum at the center of the rear between the first and fourth needles and knit 27 rounds in stockinette stitch **(GG)**.

According to the basic instructions, continue to work the **tip** in stockinette stitch in plum, only decreasing on the two needles with more stitches on the first round **(HH)** and **(II)**. Cut the working thread, pull it through the remaining stitches with the wool needle and sew.

Crochet the top edge of the slipper with 1 round of sc in plum. Work the **second slipper** in the same way, but swap the colors.

Finishing Off

Sew the threads and felt the slippers in the washing machine on the hot setting, according to the instructions (page 6). Pull into shape after washing. Stuff with paper to dry.

After drying, needle felt some dots in the contrasting color onto the top of each shoe. To do this, push a clean household sponge into the shoe. Cut off about 3" (7.6cm) of the wool, pluck off a little, and place small dots on top. Pierce the wool with the felting needle until the dots are fixed to the felted shoe.

Father's Day

Slippers with Initials

Size: Women 9–10 (UK 7–8)

Using the Heel Seam table (page 9), the slippers can also be made in other sizes. The yarn consumption would change accordingly.

Tools & Materials:
- Yarn for felting, super bulky weight
  Shown here: Wolle Rödel Strick & Filzwolle (100% virgin wool, 55 yds [50m]/1.75oz [50g]): 7.1oz (200g) in dark blue
- Circular knitting needles, US 10.5–11 (7–8mm)
- Double-pointed knitting needles, US 10.5–11 (7–8mm)
- Tapestry needle
- Orange felting wool
- Felting needle, medium or fine

Stockinette stitch: Knit stitches on the right side and purl stitches on the wrong side.

Stockinette stitch in rounds: Knit all stitches.

Gauge:
Stockinette stitch with 10.5–11 (7–8mm): 12 stitches and 16 rows = 4" x 4" (10.2 x 10.2cm), before felting; 3" x 3" (7.6 x 7.6cm), after felting.

Note: Work according to Slippers with Heel Seam (page 8).

Instructions
Using the circular knitting needle, cast on 34 stitches in dark blue (A) and, starting with one row from the right side, knit 35 rows in stockinette stitch (B), doubling the first and last stitches in the last row from the back = 36 stitches (C). Distribute the stitches evenly over four double-pointed needles (= 9 stitches per needle), close the work in the round and knit 29 rounds in stockinette stitch (D).

Work the **tip** in stockinette stitch following the basic instructions. Cut the working thread, pull it through the remaining stitches, pull it together tightly, and sew it off. Close the heel seam as described. Work the **second slipper** in the same way.

Finishing Off
Sew the threads and felt the slippers in the washing machine according to the instructions (page 6). Pull into shape after washing. Stuff with paper to dry.

After drying, needle felt the desired initials onto the top of the shoes using the felting wool and a felting needle. To do this, place the wool in the shape of the letter. Fix and compact it by constantly piercing it with the felting needle. Felt the shoes again in the washing machine.

Slippers with a Mustache

Size: Men 8–9 (UK 7–8)

Using the Heel Seam table (page 9), the slippers can also be made in other sizes. The yarn consumption would change accordingly.

Tools & Materials:

- Yarn for felting, super bulky weight
  Shown here: Wolle Rödel Strick & Filzwolle (100% virgin wool, 55 yds [50m]/1.75oz [50g]): 8.8oz (250g) in dark gray
- Yarn, super fine weight (100% cotton, 135 yds [125m]/1.75oz [50g]) in light gray
- Circular knitting needles, US 10.5–11 (7–8mm)
- Double-pointed knitting needles, US 10.5–11 (7–8mm)
- Crochet hook, US B-1 (2.25mm)
- Stuffing
- Embroidery needle and thread

Stockinette stitch: Knit stitches on the right side and purl stitches on the wrong side.

Stockinette stitch in rounds: Knit all stitches.

Gauge:

Stockinette stitch with 10.5–11 (7–8mm): 12 stitches and 16 rows = 4" x 4" (10.2 x 10.2cm), before felting; 3" x 3" (7.6 x 7.6cm), after felting.

Note: Work according to Slippers with Heel Seam (page 8).

Instructions

Using the circular knitting needle, cast on 36 stitches in dark gray **(A)**. Starting with one row from the right side, knit 37 rows in stockinette stitch **(B)**, doubling the first and last stitches in the last row from the back = 38 stitches **(C)**. Distribute the stitches over four needles of the needle set (= 9-10-9-10 sts), close the work in the round, and knit 31 rounds in stockinette stitch **(D)**.

Work the **tip** in stockinette stitch following the basic instructions. Cut the working thread, pull through the remaining stitches, pull tightly together, and sew. Close the heel seam as described. Work the **second slipper** in the same way.

Finishing Off

Sew the threads and felt the slippers in the washing machine according to the instructions (page 6). Pull into shape after washing. Stuff with paper to dry.

For the **mustache**, cast on 2 chain stitches and crochet 4 dc in the 2nd chain stitch from the hook = Round 1. Mark the beginning of the round and work in spiral rounds as follows, gradually stuffing the mustache with fiberfill:

Rounds 2–3: 4 sc each. **Round 4:** Double every 2 sts, so 2 sc in every 2 sts on the previous round (= 6 sts). **Round 5:** 6 sc. **Round 6:** Double the 1st and 4th sts each (= 8 sts). **Round 7:** Double the 1st and 5th sts each (= 10 sts). **Round 8:** Double the 1st and 6th sts each (= 12 sts). **Round 9:** Double the 1st and 12th sts each (= 14 sts). **Round 10:** Double the 1st and 4th sts each (= 16 sts). **Round 11:** Double the 1st and 5th sts each (= 18 sts). **Round 12:** 18 sc. **Round 13:** Cast off the 2nd and 3rd as well as the 6th and 7th sts together (= 16 sts). **Round 14:** Cast off the 1st and 2nd, the 5th and 6th, the 9th and 10th, and the 13th and 14th sts together (= 12 sts). **Round 15:** Cast off the 3rd and 4th as well as the 9th and 10th sts together (= 10 sts). **Round 16:** Double the 3rd and 8th sts each (= 12 sts). **Round 17:** Double the 2nd, 5th, 8th, and 11th sts each (= 16 sts). **Round 18:** Double the 4th and 7th sts each (= 18 sts). **Round 19:** 18 sc. **Round 20:** Cast off the 4th and 5th as well as the 8th and 9th sts together (= 16 sts). **Round 21:** Cast off the 4th and 5th as well as the 6th and 7th sts together (= 14 sts). **Round 22:** Cast off the 3rd and 4th as well as the 5th and 6th sts together (= 12 sts). **Round 23:** Cast off the 2nd and 3rd as well as the 4th and 5th sts together (= 10 sts). **Round 24:** Cast off the 2nd and 3rd as well as the 7th and 8th sts together (= 8 sts). **Round 25:** Cast off the 2nd and 3rd as well as the 6th and 7th sts together (= 6 sts). **Round 26:** 6 sc. **Round 27:** Cast off the 2nd and 3rd as well as the 4th and 5th sts together (= 4 sts). **Rounds 28–29:** 4 sc each.

Cut the thread, pull it through the last 4 stitches, and sew it off. Attach the mustache to the shoe with thread.

Pastel Magic

Size: Women 5–6 (UK 3–4)

Using the Heel Seam table (page 9), the slippers can also be made in other sizes. The yarn consumption would change accordingly.

Tools & Materials:

- Yarn for felting, super bulky weight
  Shown here: Lana Grossa Feltro (100% virgin wool; 55 yds [50m]/1.75oz [50g]): 3.5oz (100g) in powder pink (color 70) or green-gray (color 110), and 1.75oz (50g) in heather (color 69) or off-white (color 1), and 1.75oz (50g) in off-white (color 1) or heather (color 69)
- Knitting needles, US 10.5–11 (7–8mm)
- Double-pointed knitting needles, US 10.5–11 (7–8mm)
- Liquid latex (optional)

Gauge:

Stockinette stitch with 10.5–11 (7–8mm): 12 stitches and 16 rows = 4" x 4" (10.2 x 10.2cm), before felting; 3" x 3" (7.6 x 7.6cm), after felting.

Stockinette stitch: Knit stitches on the right side and purl stitches on the wrong side.

Stockinette stitch in rounds: Knit all stitches.

Mix and match pattern: Number of stitches divisible by 6. Work according to the chart. Every round is noted. Always repeat the pattern of 6 stitches. Always repeat Rounds 1–6.

Edge stitch: Knit the first and last stitch of each row.

Note: Work according to Slippers with Heel Seam (page 8). The colors for version 2 are in brackets.

Instructions

With the US 10.5–11 (7–8mm) circular needle, cast on 32 stitches in powder pink [green-gray] **(A)**. Work in stockinette stitch with edge stitches on both sides, starting work on the wrong side: In Rows 27 and 29, knit the 3rd and 4th stitches as well as the 3rd and 4th last stitches together = 28 stitches. At the end of Row 33 **(B)**, cast on 5 extra stitches = 33 stitches **(1 stitch less than C)**.

Join the stitches in the round and distribute them over three double-pointed needles: the newly cast-on stitches plus 6 stitches to the right and left of each = 17 stitches on needle 1, and half of the remaining stitches = 8 stitches on needles 2 and 3. Mark the round transition between needles 1 and 2.

Rounds 1–3: Knit stockinette stitch, knitting the newly cast-on stitches with purl 1 stitch, knit 1 stitch, purl 1 stitch, knit 1 stitch, purl 1 stitch. **Round 4:** In the stockinette-stitch area, increase 3 stitches evenly (= knit 1 stitch out of the cross thread) = 36 stitches. **Rounds 5–9:** Knit in stockinette stitch. **Rounds 10–18:** Work according to the knitting chart and incorporate the pattern in heather [off-white]. To do this, knit Rounds 1–6 once and Rounds 1–3 once more. Loosely lead the color you're not working along on the wrong side. **Round 19:** Cut the thread in powder pink [green-grey] and continue knitting in heather [off-white]. Knit 2 x 2 stitches together evenly spaced = 34 stitches **(C)**. **Rounds 20–23:** Stockinette stitch in heather [off-white]. **Rounds 24–27:** Stockinette stitch in off-white [powder pink] **(D)**. Then distribute the stitches on four needles = 8-9-8-9 stitches.

Work the **tip** in stockinette stitch: For the rounding, knit the 2nd and 3rd stitches together on needles 1 and 3 and the last 2nd and 3rd stitches on needles 2 and 4.

Repeat this process 6 times in total. Then close the remaining 10 stitches in the off-white [powder pink] stitch. Close the heel seam visibly in powder pink [green-gray] with the overlock stitch. Work the **second slipper** in the same way.

Finishing Off

Weave in the loose ends and felt the slippers in the washing machine on the warm setting, according to the instructions (page 6). Pull into shape after washing. Stuff with paper to dry.

Optional: Coat the soles with liquid latex to achieve an anti-slip effect.

Mix and Match Chart

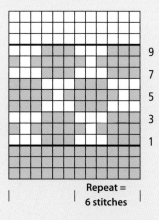

Repeat =
6 stitches

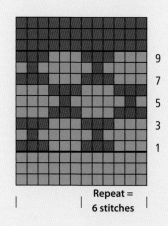

Repeat =
6 stitches

▨ = 1 stockinette stitch in green-gray
☐ = 1 stockinette stitch in off-white
▨ = 1 stockinette stitch in powder pink
▨ = 1 stockinette stitch in heather

Mary Janes

Size: Kids 2–3.5 and Women 5–7 (UK 13.5–5)

The information for Kids 2–3 (UK 13.5–2) is in front of the brackets; the information for Kids 3.5 and Women 5 (UK 2.5–3) is in brackets, before the slash; information for Women 6–7 (UK 4–5) is in brackets, after the slash. If there is only one specification, it applies to all sizes.

Tools & Materials:
- Yarn for felting, super bulky weight
  Shown here: Lana Grossa Feltro (100% virgin wool; 55 yds [50m]/1.75oz [50g]): 5.3oz (150g) in mottled beige (color 24)
- Double-pointed knitting needles, US 10.5–11 (7–8mm)
- Elastic band in rose gold, 10" x 2" (25.4 x 5.1cm)
- Liquid latex (optional)

Gauge:
Stockinette stitch with 10.5–11 (7–8mm): 12 stitches and 16 rows = 4" x 4" (10.2 x 10.2cm), before felting; 3" x 3" (7.6 x 7.6cm), after felting.

Stockinette stitch: Knit stitches on the right side and purl stitches on the wrong side.

Stockinette stitch in rounds: Knit all stitches.

Instructions

Cast on 28 [29/30] stitches and work 1 row of purl stitches (wrong side). Leave the cast-on thread hanging long and use it later to sew it together. Knit 26 [28/30] rows in stockinette stitch. In Row 27 [29/31], knit 2 stitches together on both sides = 26 [27/28] stitches. Repeat these decreases on Rows 33 and 37 = 22 [23/24] stitches.

At the end of Row 41 [43/45], do not turn, but cast on 8 more stitches and close all stitches in the round = 30 [31/32] stitches. Distribute the stitches to 7-8-7-8 [7-8-8-8/8-8-8-8] stitches on four double-pointed needles and work 8 [10/12] rounds in stockinette stitch.

For the **tip**, work the 2nd and 3rd stitches together on needles 1 and 3, and the last 2nd and 3rd stitches on the needles 2 and 4. Repeat these decreases 4 more times [5 times/5 times]. Then cut the thread, pull it through the remaining 10 [7/8] stitches, pull it together tightly and sew it off.

Close the heel seam as described in the basic instructions on page 8. Work the **second slipper** in the same way.

Finishing Off

Weave in the loose ends and felt the slippers in the washing machine on the warm setting, according to the instructions (page 6). Pull into shape after washing. Stuff with paper to dry.

Cut two elastic bands of 4" [4 ¼"/4 ¾"] (10.2 [10.8/12.1cm]) each. Using a ½" (1.3cm) seam allowance on both sides, this leaves 2 ¾" [3 ⅛"/3 ½"] (7 [7.9/8.9cm]) for the band. Measure 3 ½" [4"/4 ¼"] (8.9 [10.2/10.8cm]) from the center back at the upper edge of the shoe, and sew on the elastic band over 2" (5.1cm) from there toward the toe. Fold the seam allowance to the inside.

Optional: Coat the soles with liquid latex to achieve an anti-slip effect.

Ballerinas

Size: Kids 2–3.5 and Women 5–7 (UK 13.5–5)

The information for Kids 2–3 (UK 13.5–2) is in front of the brackets; the information for Kids 3.5 and Women 5 (UK 2.5–3) is in brackets, before the slash; information for Women 6–7 (UK 4–5) is in brackets, after the slash. If there is only one specification, it applies to all sizes.

Tools & Materials:

- Yarn for felting, super bulky weight
  Shown here: Lana Grossa Feltro (100% virgin wool; 55 yds [50m]/1.75oz [50g]): 5.3oz (150g) in powder pink (color 70)
- Double-pointed knitting needles, US 10.5–11 (7–8mm)
- Single hole punch
- 2 satin shoelaces in pink, 40" (101.6cm) long
- Liquid latex (optional)

Gauge:
Stockinette stitch with 10.5–11 (7–8mm): 12 stitches and 16 rows = 4" x 4" (10.2 x 10.2cm), before felting; 3" x 3" (7.6 x 7.6cm), after felting.

Stockinette stitch: Knit stitches on the right side and purl stitches on the wrong side.

Stockinette stitch in rounds: Knit all stitches.

Edge stitch: Knit the first and last stitch of each row.

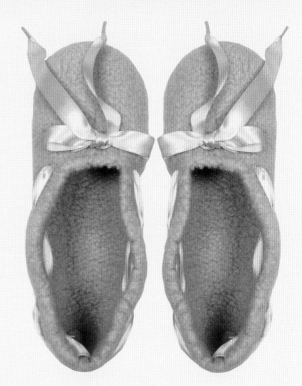

Instructions

Cast on 28 [29/30] stitches and work 1 row of purl stitches (wrong side). Leave the cast-on thread hanging long and use it later to sew it together. Knit 26 [28/30] rows in stockinette stitch. In Row 27 [29/31], knit 2 stitches together on each side = 26 [27/28] stitches. Repeat these decreases on Rows 33 and 37 = 22 [23/24] stitches.

At the end of Row 41 [43/45], do not turn, but cast on 8 more stitches and close all stitches in the round = 30 [31/32] stitches. Distribute the stitches to 7-8-7-8 [7-8-8-8/8-8-8-8] stitches on four double-pointed needles and work 8 [10/12] rounds in stockinette stitch.

Knit the 2nd and 3rd stitches together for the **tip** on needles 1 and 3, and the 2nd and 3rd last stitches together on needles 2 and 4. Repeat these decreases 4 more times [5 times/5 times]. Cut the thread, pull it through the remaining 10 [7/8] stitches, pull it together tightly, and sew it off.

Close the heel seam as described. Work the **second slipper** in the same way.

Finishing Off

Weave in the loose ends and felt the slippers in the washing machine on the warm setting, according to the instructions (page 6). Pull into shape after washing. Stuff with paper to dry.

Use the hole punch to evenly distribute the holes: punch one hole each in the center back on the right and left of the seam, one each on the right and left across the corner of the front cut-out, and three more holes at even intervals between these holes on the side edges. Punch them ½" (1.3cm) below the edge. Pull a satin ribbon through each hole , tying the laces into a bow at the front.

Optional: Coat the soles with liquid latex to achieve an anti-slip effect.

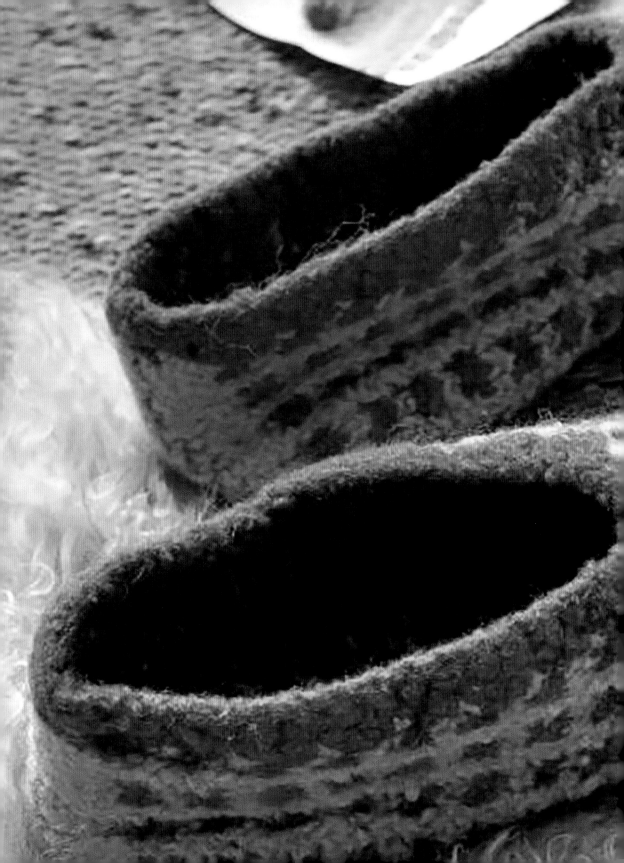

Checks in Blue

Size: Men 8–9 (UK 7–8)

Using the Heel Seam table (page 9), the slippers can also be made in other sizes. The yarn consumption would change accordingly.

Tools & Materials:
- Yarn for felting, bulky weight
  Shown here: buttinette Wool Butt Felting Wool (100% virgin wool, 55 yds [50m]/1.75oz [50g]): 3.5oz (100g) each in light blue (color 99.129.65) and blue (color 99.219.34)
- Circular knitting needles, US 10.5–11 (7–8mm)
- Double-pointed knitting needles, US 10.5–11 (7–8mm)
- Crochet hook, US L-11 (8mm)

Slip stitch pattern in rows: Number of stitches divisible by 3 + 3 stitches.
   Row 1 (Right Side): Knit all stitches with light blue. **Row 2 (Wrong Side):** Knit all stitches. **Row 3:** With blue, knit 1 stitch, slip 1 stitch with the yarn behind the work as for purl knitting, *knit 2 stitches, slip 1 stitch with the yarn behind the work as for purl knitting, repeat from * onward, and knit 1 stitch. **Row 4:** Knit 1 stitch, slip 1 stitch with the yarn in front of the work as for purl knitting, *knit 2 stitches, slip 1 stitch with the yarn in front of the work as for purl knitting, repeat from * onward, and knit 1 stitch.

Slip stitch pattern in rounds: Number of stitches divisible by 3.
   Rounds 1–2: Knit all stitches with light blue.
Round 3: Knit 2 stitches with blue, *slip 1 stitch with the yarn behind the work as for purl knitting, and repeat from * onward. **Round 4:** *Purl 2 stitches, with the thread behind the work, slip 1 stitch as if to purl, and repeat from * onward.

Stockinette stitch in rounds: Knit all stitches.

Gauge:
Stockinette stitch with 10.5–11 (7–8mm): 12 stitches and 16 rows = 4" x 4" (10.2 x 10.2cm), before felting; 3" x 3" (7.6 x 7.6cm), after felting.
   Note: Work according to Slippers with Heel Seam (page 8).

Instructions

With US 10.5–11 (7–8mm) circular needles, cast on 36 stitches in light blue **(A)** and knit 37 rows in slip stitch pattern **(B)**, starting on the right side and doubling the first and last stitch when working the wrong side = 38 stitches **(C)**. Distribute the stitches on four needles (= 9-10-9-10 sts). Close the work in the round, cast on 1 stitch at the beginning of the 1 needle for the slip stitch pattern (= 39 stitches). Work the increases to match the slip stitch pattern so that the repeat is correct again. Work 31 rounds in a slip stitch pattern **(D)**.

Work the **tip** in stockinette stitch according to the basic instructions in either light blue or blue: in each round, knit the first 2 stitches of each needle together until there are only 10 stitches left. Note: Depending on the sizes, there can only be 8 stitches at this point. Cut the working thread, pull it through the remaining stitches, pull it together tightly, and sew it off. Close the heel seam as described.

Crochet the top edge with 1 round of sc in blue. Work the **second slipper** in the same way.

Finishing Off

Sew the threads and felt the slippers in the washing machine on the hot setting, according to the instructions (page 6). Pull into shape after washing. Stuff with paper to dry.

Sweet Kitten

Size: Women 5–6 (UK 3–4)

Using the Heel Seam table (page 9), the slippers can also be made in other sizes. The yarn consumption would change accordingly.

Tools & Materials:

- Yarn for felting, super bulky weight
  Shown here: Lana Grossa Feltro (100% virgin wool; 55 yds [50m]/1.75oz [50g]): 3.5oz (100g) in mottled gray (color 3) and 5.3oz (150g) mottled dark gray (color 4)
- Double-pointed knitting needles, US 10.5–11 (7–8mm)
- Crochet hooks, US J-10 (6mm) and M/N-13 (9mm)
- Felting needle, medium
- 4 animal eyes in brown, 12mm diameter
- Liquid latex (optional)

Stockinette stitch: Knit stitches on the right side and purl stitches on the wrong side.

Stockinette stitch in rounds: Knit all stitches.

Stripe sequence: *2 rows/rounds of mottled dark gray, 2 rows/rounds of mottled gray, and repeat from * onward.

Knotted edge stitch: Knit both edge stitches on the right and wrong sides.

Gauge:
Stockinette stitch with 10.5–11 (7–8mm): 12 stitches and 16 rows = 4" x 4" (10.2 x 10.2cm), before felting; 3" x 3" (7.6 x 7.6cm), after felting.

   Note: Work according to Slippers with Heel Seam (page 8).

Instructions

Using the circular knitting needle, cast on 30 stitches in mottled dark gray (A) and knit 31 rows in stockinette stitch and in the stripe sequence, starting work on the wrong side. Work the first and last stitch of each row as a knot edge stitch. On the last row on the wrong side, knit 1 stitch after the 1st stitch and 1 stitch before the last stitch from the cross yarn (= 32 stitches) (C).

Distribute the stitches over four needles on the double-pointed needles (= 8 stitches per needle). Join the piece in the round and knit in stockinette stitch: continue the stripe sequence for 12 more rounds, then 13 rounds in mottled gray = 25 rounds from the end of the round (D).

Work the **tip** in stockinette stitch in mottled gray according to the basic instructions (E). For the rounding on each round, knit the first 2 stitches on each needle together until only 8 (or 10 stitches depending on size) remain (F) and (G). Cut the working thread, pull it through the remaining stitches, pull it together tightly, and sew it off. Close the heel seam as described. Work the **second slipper** in the same way.

Finishing Off

Weave in the loose ends and felt the slippers in the washing machine on the warm setting, according to the instructions (page 6). Pull into shape after washing. Stuff with paper to dry.

Ears (work 4 times): Form a magic ring in mottled gray. Work with the US 10 (6mm) crochet hook as follows:

Round 1: 1 ch, 3 sc in the thread ring. **Round 2:** 1 turning ch, 1 sc, 3 sc in the following stitch, 1 sc = 5 sc. **Round 3:** 1 turning ch, 2 sc, 3 sc in the following stitch, 2 sc = 7 sc. **Round 4:** 1 turning ch, 7 sc. Finish the work. Sew two ears to the head of each slipper.

Tail (work 2 times): 8 ch + 1 turning ch in mottled dark gray, cast on double strands with US 13 (9mm) crochet hook, and crochet 8 sl sts back. Finish the work. Sew a tail to the center back of each slipper.

Felt the nose in a circle using the mottled dark gray yarn and a felting needle. Felt three whiskers on each side of the nose in mottled dark gray, twist up the ends of the thread, and do not felt them. Felt the mouth in a line with the felting needle in mottled dark gray. Sew on the eyes.

Optional: Coat the soles with liquid latex to achieve an anti-slip effect.

Little Bear

Pictured on pages 82–83.

Size: Kids 1.5–2 (UK 13–13.5)

Using the Heel Seam table (page 9), the slippers can also be made in other sizes. The yarn consumption would change accordingly.

Tools & Materials:

- Yarn for felting, super bulky weight
  Shown here: Lana Grossa Feltro (100% virgin wool; 55 yds [50m]/1.75oz [50g]): 5.3oz (150g) in brown (color 23) and 1.75oz (50g) mottled gray (color 3)
- Double-pointed knitting needles, US 10.5–11 (7–8mm)
- Crochet hooks, US J-10 (6mm) and M/N-13 (9mm)
- Felting needle, medium
- 4 animal eyes in black, 6mm diameter
- Mottled dark gray wool yarn
- Liquid latex (optional)

Stockinette stitch: Knit stitches on the right side and purl stitches on the wrong side.

Stockinette stitch in rounds: Knit all stitches.

Knotted edge stitch: Knit both edge stitches on the right and wrong sides.

Gauge:

Stockinette stitch with 10.5–11 (7–8mm): 12 stitches and 16 rows = 4" x 4" (10.2 x 10.2cm), before felting; 3" x 3" (7.6 x 7.6cm), after felting.

   Note: Work according to Slippers with Heel Seam (page 8).

Instructions

Using the circular knitting needle, cast on 28 stitches in brown (**A**) and knit 27 rows in stockinette stitch = 2 rows more than (**B**), starting work on the wrong side. Work the first and last stitches of each row as a knotted edge stitch. On the last row on the wrong side, knit 1 stitch after the first stitch and 1 stitch before the last stitch from the cross yarn = 30 stitches (**C**). Distribute the stitches on four needles (= 7-8-7-8 stitches per needle). Join the piece in the round and knit 23 rounds in stockinette stitch (**D**).

Work the **tip** in stockinette stitch brown according to the basic instructions. To make the curve, knit the first 2 stitches on each needle together on each round until there are only 10 stitches left (or 8 stitches depending on size). Cut the working thread, pull it through the remaining stitches, pull it together tightly, and sew it off. Close the heel seam as described. Work the **second slipper** in the same way.

Finishing Off

Weave in the loose ends and felt the slippers in the washing machine on the warm setting, according to the instructions (page 6). Pull into shape after washing. Stuff with paper to dry.

Ears (work 4 times): Form a magic ring in mottled gray. Work with the US 10 (6mm) crochet hook as follows:

Round 1: 1 chain ch, 6 sc in the thread ring.
Rounds 2–4: 1 turning ch, 6 sc. Finish the work. Sew two ears to the head of each slipper.

Tail (work 2 times): Cast on 6 ch + 1 turning ch in mottled gray double crochet with a US 13 (9mm) crochet hook and crochet back 6 sl st. Finish the work. Sew a tail to the center back of each slipper.

Felt the nose in a circle using the mottled dark gray felting needle. Felt the mouth in a line with the felting needle in mottled dark gray. Sew on the eyes.

Optional: Coat the soles with liquid latex to achieve an anti-slip effect.

Happy Bunny

Size: all sizes, see Heel Seam table (page 9)

Tools & Materials:

- Yarn for felting, super bulky weight
  Shown here: Lana Grossa Feltro (100% virgin wool; 55 yds [50m]/1.75oz [50g]): off-white (color 1) amount depending on slipper size, and 1.75oz (50g) off-white (color 1)
- Double-pointed knitting needles, US 10.5–11 (7–8mm)
- Mottled gray, dusty pink, and black wool yarn
- Tapestry needle
- Pom-pom maker
- Liquid latex (optional)

Moss stitch: Knit 1 stitch, purl 1 stitch alternately. Stagger the pattern by 1 stitch on each row/round.

Gauge:

Stockinette stitch with 10.5–11 (7–8mm): 12 stitches and 16 rows = 4" x 4" (10.2 x 10.2cm), before felting; 3" x 3" (7.6 x 7.6cm), after felting.

Note: Work according to Slippers with Heel Seam (page 8).

Instructions

Knit one pair of slippers in off-white according to the basic instructions; however, do not work in stockinette stitch but in moss stitch. Close the heel seam as described and work the second slipper in the same way.

For the **ears (work 4 times)**, cast on 9 stitches and knit 9 rows in moss stitch, starting with a row on the wrong side. Then knit 2 times the first 2 stitches together in each row = 7 stitches and knit 2 times the first and last 2 stitches together = 3 stitches. Cut the thread and pull it through the remaining stitches. Fold the ears slightly inward at the base and sew them onto the shoe.

For the **nose**, embroider in satin stitch over the toe of the shoe using dusty pink. For the **whiskers**, thread 3 mottled gray threads underneath the nose so that about 4" (10.2cm) of thread hangs on the right and left.

Eyes (work 4 times): Form a large knot with black using a tapestry needle, and thicken it by piercing it several times until you have a ball about ½" (1.3cm) thick. Sew on the eyes.

Finishing Off

Weave in the loose ends and felt the slippers in the washing machine on the warm setting, according to the instructions (page 6). Pull into shape after washing. Stuff with paper to dry.

For the **tail (work 2 times)**, wrap a pom-pom with a 1 ½" (3.8cm) diameter in off-white. After the slippers have dried, sew one tail on each of the shoes about ¾" (1.9cm) below the edge to the back of the shoes.

Optional: Coat the soles with liquid latex to achieve an anti-slip effect.

Puppy Slippers

Pictured on page 89.

Size: all sizes, see Heel Seam table (page 9)

Tools & Materials:

- Yarn for felting, super bulky weight
  Shown here: Lana Grossa Feltro (100% virgin
  wool; 55 yds [50m]/1.75oz [50g]): cognac
  (color 77) amount depending on slipper size,
  and 1.75oz (50g) off-white (color 1)
- Double-pointed knitting needles, US 10.5–11
  (7–8mm)
- Black wool yarn
- Tapestry needle
- Pom-pom maker
- Liquid latex (optional)

Stockinette stitch: Knit stitches on the right side
and purl stitches on the wrong side.

Stockinette stitch in rounds: Knit all stitches.

Stripe sequence: Knit 6 rows/rounds of cognac and
1 row/round of off-white alternately.

Knitting pattern: Number of stitches divisible by 6.
Before starting the knitting pattern, adjust the
number of stitches accordingly by increasing or
decreasing, and change back to the original number
of stitches after the 6 rounds. Work according to the
counting pattern. Work Rounds 1–6 once.

Gauge:
Stockinette stitch with 10.5–11 (7–8mm): 12 stitches
and 16 rows = 4"" x 4" (10.2 x 10.2cm), before felting;
3" x 3" (7.6 x 7.6cm), after felting.

   Note: Work according to Slippers with Heel Seam
(page 8).

5

3

1

| 6 stitches |

■ = 1 stockinette stitch in cognac

□ = 1 stockinette stitch in off-white

Instructions

Knit one pair of slippers according to the basic instructions: Cast on the required number of stitches in off-white and work in stockinette stitch in the stripe sequence, starting with a row on the wrong side. At 6 rounds before the start of the tip, work the knitting pattern according to the chart.

The knitting pattern requires a number of stitches divisible by 6. If there are fewer or more stitches (depending on the size), increase or decrease the missing stitches before the tip and then decrease or increase again accordingly. Knit Rounds 1–6 once.

Continue working in off-white and finish the tip according to the basic instructions. Close the heel seam as described and work the **second slipper** in the same way.

For the **ears (work 4 times)**, cast on 7 stitches in cognac and knit 5 rows in stockinette stitch, starting with a row from the on the wrong side. Knit the first 2 stitches together on each row until there are only 3 stitches left on the needle. Cut the thread and pull it through the remaining stitches. Fold the ears slightly inward at the base and sew them onto the shoe.

For the **nose**, embroider in a satin stitch over the toe of the shoe using black.

For the **eyes (work 4 times)**, form a large knot with black using a tapestry needle and thicken it by piercing it several times until you have a ball about ½" (1.3cm) thick. Sew the eyes to the tip of the points in the white field.

Finishing Off

Weave in the loose ends and felt the slippers in the washing machine on the warm setting, according to the instructions (page 6). Pull into shape after washing. Stuff with paper to dry.

Optional: Coat the soles with liquid latex to achieve an anti-slip effect.

Love Bug

Size: Women 5–6 (UK 3–4)

Using the Heel Seam table (page 9), the slippers can also be made in other sizes. The yarn consumption would change accordingly.

Tools & Materials:
- Yarn for felting, super bulky weight
  Shown here: Lana Grossa Feltro (100% virgin wool; 55 yds [50m]/1.75oz [50g]): 3.5oz (100g) in red (color 7), and 1.75oz (50g) in black (color 6)
- Off-white wool yarn
- Circular knitting needles, US 10.5–11 (7–8mm)
- Double-pointed knitting needles, US 10.5–11 (7–8mm)
- Crochet hook, US K-10 ½ (6.5mm)
- Tapestry needle

Stockinette stitch: Knit stitches on the right side and purl stitches on the wrong side.

Stockinette stitch in rounds: Knit all stitches.

Gauge:
Stockinette stitch with 10.5–11 (7–8mm): 12 stitches and 16 rows = 4" x 4" (10.2 x 10.2cm), before felting; 3" x 3" (7.6 x 7.6cm), after felting.

   Note: Work according to Slippers with Heel Seam (page 8).

Instructions

Knit a pair of slippers in red following the basic instructions, continuing from the beginning of the point in black: With the US 10.5–11 (7–8mm) circular knitting needle, cast on 30 stitches in red **(A)** and knit 31 rows in stockinette stitch **(B)**, doubling the first and last stitches in the last row on the wrong side = 32 stitches **(C)**. Distribute the stitches on four needles (8 stitches per needle), join the work in the round, and knit 25 rounds in stockinette stitch **(D)**.

Cut the thread in red and work the **tip** with black according to the basic instructions: In each round, knit the first 2 stitches of each needle together until there are only 8 stitches left. Note: Depending on the size, there can also be 10 stitches at this point. Cut the thread and pull it through the remaining stitches.

Crochet a **black line** of slip stitches in the center of the foot. It begins at the transition from black tip to red foot.

For a **spot (work 10 times)**, crochet 11 dc in a magic ring, starting with 3 chain stitches and close with 1 slip stitch to form a round. Cut the thread long and use it to sew on. Crochet 5 dots per shoe and sew them onto the shoe.

Embroider two **eyes** in off-white onto the black tip. Embroider a small black pupil in the middle. Close the back heel seam as described. Work the **second slipper** in the same way.

Finishing Off

Sew the threads and felt the slippers in the washing machine on the hot setting, according to the instructions (page 6). Pull into shape after washing. Stuff with paper to dry.

INDEX

Note: Page numbers in *italics* indicated projects. Page numbers in parentheses indicate photos prior to project instructions.

A

abbreviations, stitch, 2
Autumn Leaves, *(28–29)*, *30–31*

B

Ballerinas, *76–77*
bear slippers, *(82–83)*, *86–87*
Blue and Purple with Polka Dots, *(60–61)*, *62–63*
bunny slippers, *88–89*
Buttoned Up, *(36–37)*, *38–39*

C

cap heel, slippers with, 10–11
Checks in Blue, *(78–79)*, *80–81*
Cheeky, Cheerful, Colorful, *(32–33)*, *34–35*

F

Father's Day
    Pastel Magic, *70–71*
    Slippers with a Mustache, *(65)*, *66–67*
    Slippers with Initials, *64–65*

G

gauge, 5–6, 8, 10. **See also specific projects**

H

Happy Bunny, *88–89*
heel (cap), slippers with, 10–11
heel seam, slippers with, 8–9

I

Inspired by Asia, *(18–19)*, *20–23*

K

kitten slippers, *84–85*
knit felting
    about: keeping pieces separated, 7; process, 5–7
    knitting needle for, 5
    needle felting, 7
    sizing slippers, 7
    slippers with heel seam, 8–9
    useful tips, 7
    in washing machine, 6–7
    yarn for, 5
knitting needle, 5

L

liquid latex on slipper soles, 7
Little Bear, *86–87*
Love Bug, *92–94*

M

Mary Janes, *(72–73)*, *74–75*

N

needle, knitting, 5
needle felting, 7

P

Pastel Magic, *(68–69)*
projects
    about: gauge, 5–6, 8, 10 (**see also specific projects**); liquid latex on soles, 7; overview of, 3; size charts, 9, 11; slippers with cap heel, 10–11; slippers with heel seam, 8–9
    Autumn Leaves, *(28–29)*, *30–31*
    Ballerinas, *76–77*
    Blue and Purple with Polka Dots, *(60–61)*, *62–63*
    Buttoned Up, *(36–37)*, *38–39*
    Checks in Blue, *(78–79)*, *80–81*
    Cheeky, Cheerful, Colorful, *(32–33)*, *34–35*
    Father's Day Pastel Magic, *(68–69)*, *70–71*
    Father's Day Slippers with a Mustache, *(65)*, *66–67*
    Father's Day Slippers with Initials, *64–65*
    Happy Bunny, *88–89*
    Inspired by Asia, *(18–19)*, *20–23*
    Little Bear, *(82–83)*, *86–87*
    Love Bug, *92–94*
    Mary Janes, *(72–73)*, *74–75*
    Puppy Slippers, *(89)*, *90–91*
    Softly Striped, *(22–23)*, *24–25*
    Sophisticated Checks, *(56–57)*, *58–59*
    Spotty Slipper, *(14–15)*, *16–19*
    A Star is Born, *44–47*
    Stylish Understatement, *26–27*
    Sweet Kitten, *(82–83)*, *84–85*
    Tone on Tone, *(48–49)*, *50–51*
    Triple Mélange, *54–55*
    Warm, Warmer, Warmest, *(40–41)*, *42–43*
Puppy Slippers, *(89)*, *90–91*

S

size charts, 9, 11
sizing slippers, 7
Softly Striped, *(22–23)*, *24–25*
Sophisticated Checks, *(56–57)*, *58–59*
Spotty Slipper, *(14–15)*, *16–19*
A Star is Born, *44–47*
Stylish Understatement, *26–27*
Sweet Kitten, *(82–83)*, *84–85*

T

Tone on Tone, *(48–49)*, *50–51*
Triple Mélange, *54–55*

W

Warm, Warmer, Warmest, *(40–41)*, *42–43*
washing machine, felting in, 6–7

Y

yarn, 5

Knitting and Felting Slippers

Landauer Publishing, www.landauerpub.com, is an imprint of Fox Chapel Publishing Company, Inc.

© Christophorus Verlag in der Christian Verlag GmbH, Munich, Germany

Knitting and Felting Slippers is a translation of the 2023 version originally published in German by Christophorus Verlag under the title *Hauschuhe Stricken & Filzen* in Munich, Germany. This version is published by Landauer, an imprint of Fox Chapel Publishing Company, Inc.

Fox Chapel Publishing Team
Managing Editor: Gretchen Bacon
Acquisitions Editor: Amelia Johanson
Translator: Freire Disseny + Comunicació
Editor: Christa Oestreich
Designer: Freire Disseny + Comunicació
Proofreader: Kurt Conley
Indexer: Jay Kreider

Christophorus Verlag Team
Authors: Sabine Abel, pp. 22–39, 48–51, 60–63, 78–81; Annette Diepolder, pp. 64–67; Karoline Hoffmeister, pp. 14–17, 40–47, 52–59, 68–77, 88–94; Sabine Ruf, 18–21, 82–83
Project Management: Maria Möllenkamp
Cover Design: Regina Degenkolbe
Photos & Styling: Elisabeth Berkau, pp. 2, 4, 12–13, 18–19, 22–63, 68–63; Herbert Dehn, pp. 14–15; Hermann Mareth, pp. 64–67

ISBN 978-1-63981-102-1

Library of Congress Control Number: 2024942562

To learn more about the other great books from Fox Chapel Publishing,
or to find a retailer near you, call toll-free 800-457-9112,
send mail to
903 Square Street,
Mount Joy, PA 17552,
or visit us at www.FoxChapelPublishing.com.

We are always looking for talented authors. To submit an idea, please send a brief inquiry to acquisitions@foxchapelpublishing.com.

Printed in China
First printing